RIPPING DOWN HALF THE TREES

THE HUGH MACLENNAN POETRY SERIES
Editors: Allan Hepburn and Carolyn Smart

Ripping down half the trees

EVAN J

McGill-Queen's University Press
Montreal & Kingston • London • Chicago

ISBN 978-0-2280-0546-9 (paper)
ISBN 978-0-2280-0743-2 (ePDF)
ISBN 978-0-2280-0744-9 (ePUB)

Legal deposit second quarter 2021
Bibliothèque nationale du Québec

Printed in Canada on acid-free paper that is 100% ancient forest free
(100% post-consumer recycled), processed chlorine free

Financé par le   Funded by the   Conseil des arts   Canada Council
gouvernement   Government   du Canada   for the Arts
du Canada   of Canada

We acknowledge the support of the Canada Council for the Arts.

Nous remercions le Conseil des arts du Canada de son soutien.

Library and Archives Canada Cataloguing in Publication

Title: Ripping down half the trees / Evan J.

Names: J, Evan, author.

Series: Hugh MacLennan poetry series.

Description: Series statement: The Hugh MacLennan poetry series

Identifiers: Canadiana (print) 20210169850 | Canadiana (ebook)
    20210169893 | ISBN 9780228005469 (softcover) |
    ISBN 9780228007432 (PDF) | ISBN 9780228007449 (ePUB)

Subjects: LCGFT: Poetry.

Classification: LCC PS8619.A2 R57 2021 | DDC C811/.6—dc23

This book was typeset by Marquis Interscript in 9.5/13 Sabon.

CONTENTS

THE METRO

BLOOR-YONGE

for Dionne Brand

This Friday ropes 'em together,
the gorgeous-scarved,
the bros, the packs, the slow,
the struts, the flocks, those maddened to escalator.
They're translating, transferring,
hours through boxes, through boxes,
through oblong boxes, we are
within tunnels.

But some always jam in transition, like I,
and it's here that we transcribe the city.
We log you in passing,
track panics, hint sex,
note the blank passive everyones,
etch your heaviest everyday sinking-sinuses,
check the vacant, the dying.

We catalogue you on these tiles,
city and your sadnesses,
hauling so much life on biceps,
sore backs, bare feet, iTunes.
Within skins and nails old acrylic,
through perms and poisonous shadows,
the colour is always grey.
Down here the lights are always off,
but you know, the eyes adjust.

In the dark down here
that grey is afloat.
It swings between columns
stroking every coloured arm.
It spends the nights brushing hair,
dusting lipgloss, unwinging late-night lash aesthetics.
For some it twirls into iris
then curtsies a tear just for smudging away.
Eyes sliver so not to feel soft caresses
but through slits, wanting-stares catch the bareness.

If you're stuck you will see all this.

Endless broken phone calls.
The bellowing-heft of "the fuck!?,"
the always bawling of lovers unable to escape,
partners bungeeing back.
And the full-timer subway hustlers,
sad eyes in a spiel but still truly the suffering, always
in hunger, in pleas to the masses
exclaiming in grey:

Can someone
please help me
with somethin'
to eat?

Can someone
please help me
with somethin'
to eat?

Can someone
please help me
with somethin'
to eat?

Can someone
please help me?

Nine at night
all the poverty-line serfs
funnel underground from escalator
spouting eyes broke from counting tills until
they finger the bones of caribou in quarters.
What ruined citizens, investment pedestrians
spoiled with EarPods and banknotes,
Instagram ad glasses erasing memory
of motion to sidestep a speedbump
sleeping bag above subway vent kindling
upon rainy sidewalk. And a lord above,
the speckled white crosswalk man
will brand you, burn your cones,
and in forever's next five minutes
he will be imprinted upon this world.
Expect this to repeat until we question
the beauty of repetition.
For the man inside the bedsheet hurdle
the irony of home
lives within the phrase
"tripped up,"
and the mockery
of the sodden moment remains
his thirst
which is to say, humanity.
Above him, the fashion depots deflate,
the house music meant to panhandle purchases
from cataleptic customers
flickers off, replaced by a fluorescent sizzle that

licks at the ringing emptiness
settling like a fog upon the x-ing allure
of the Dundas four-way.
The gravity of intersection.
This is the moment I await,
the time when capital slaves are released to sleep,
the time to spot Drake with all his feelings
climbing to mount the capitol phallus of the Ron.

IF HOMELESSNESS IS A SANDWICH,
OUR CULTURE OF SILENCE IS THE BREAD

If bank windows only mirror
a jekyll post-chrysalis,
and the Hamilton sidewalk
flips its suit inside out, vampires
bearding into werewolves and
you've nowhere to shave, it's near
impossible to retain your quarters
past the rush of the hour.

Hence all the rubbish,
cotton sleeves and runaways
jammed like PB between
rotten Mercedes SUVs lined up
at every downtown light on King Street.
With all the breadless appendages palm up,
I'm gunna have to ask you
for no words about what is seen
in a city's creases and crust.

But even in silence, I'm guessing
you still feel the sides
and solutions of the issue
knocking about like legs
in a public hot tub,
kneecaps bumping thighs,
and we're all too civil
to tell each other:
that's sexy, I like that, or
back the fuck off, old man.

ALL THE FRIENDS AT THE PARTY

Do not become enamoured of power
Michel Foucault

How black must someone paint a face
for a nation's denizens to demand
the Sussex home be burned to ground?

I don't ever watch the news
but I can still picture his pale bulb blinkers
in darkest closets of the common house.

Imagine all the repeat times
the honest janitor was asked
to leave those deepest nooks unswept.

In country school attic
elves and dog tally origins:

Wīnipēk, a Cree word
for cloudy water, a silt-rich red lake.

Gimlé, a Norse heaven
where gods live when worlds end.

From the airport turned dragway
there's a summer weekend rumbling
that's equal parts funny-car

to Hells Angels Harley.
The roar is the repute of Gimli,
is the rift from the old ways

from volcanoes to flatlanders,
from Althing to Tergesen's,
from Eddas to coffee

black like sheep's blood.
The shift is how marauders are made,
entrepreneurs local-born

from folx with Ammas
who call wealth a smoked goldeye.
It's why the plaster was laid

for the seaside Viking statue
and the Highway 9 motel bar
grimy with VLTs and cheap rye.

This grand turn of capital
gets called Icelandic pride
and you can smell it

like mash on the wind,
like piles of fishflies rotting
beneath a July lamppost.

I know all this because
my eyes and lines shadow
a dóttir of elves

swimming above zebras
as the sun bursts its rise
like a greenback from Lake Winnipeg's water.

Icelanders must always swallow
the violent eruptions of the orange hour
and push themselves

to opportunity in the waves
past the ironwood
of Willow Point.

This digital water
falls of every nation flying
selfie stick flag pole.
Bank accounts tumbling
over. You
don't come here for grandmother
river. Is this
desecration? No. No,
look. The magic
inside Niagara horseshoe is water
rising the crags
up to kiss as
mist,
and it is only today's one naked
body, the baby,
that loves water
candidly.

JUST OVER THE MOUNTAIN FROM YAQUI, ARIZONA

Highway 66 traffics fortune
on a jammed entry dirt drive
to the desert hotel in Oatman.
Colonizer donkeys and gunslingers
compete for portraits of ministers.
The bellboys and burros
usher the mainstreet snowbirds
behind corrals spruced for viewing.
A gaudy mayor topped with red
cowboy fez pistols blanks at
the Western Union for Shriners donations.
The snowbirds advance chuckles
paying for smiles with fiscal handouts.
This is what tips me off, the insinuations so
federal, the bills like PR pamphlets
of a prejudice sitting just behind
all these false fronts.
And I don't see regret in anyone. The charity
and councillors so eager to crumple notes
out of sight. But every extra dollar
pocketed in this town finds pride
and re-emerges to paper
the hotel-restaurant walls.
Ten thousand Washington green eyes
helping insulate while blue-nosed
Canadian tenders are plucked,
the Lauriers used for cleaning.
It is rare that fortunes ever add up.
Every bit in the mouth of Oatman
is obtuse.

INVADERS: MYSTERY SPACE RIDERS
OR, AN ODE TO ALAN KURDI

You arrive in past tense. You hold brother, mother
and all the pieces of your father's heart
in your palming hands.
You are boyness, you are endurance, you are oil
aflame on the ocean until every susurration is respired.

To write this poem, tears must wet my fingers and spark
    a keyboard.
I am shocked with every keying
but I've been taught never to move.
Poets, we are cowards,
we could not have helped you,
we are the mortar jammed under words
submerged by bricks of language,
we will not stop a tank or the terrorism of teeth
and our rhythm will not help you float.
None of us could spot a fake life jacket from the real,
we would all have died before you
but you should not have died,
you should not have died, and we should never stop crying.

You should learn what killed you:
it was hope in the night lights of Kos only four kilometres
    away,
it was wind and the tumult of that perilous straight,
it was a hard boat still crushed in the waves,
it was traffickers shit out of luck,
it was your father with no other options,
it was Poseidon erect and irate,

it was Assad, Abu Fadi, al-Baghdadi, Erdoğan, Obama,
    Putin,
it was Harper-Trudeau in electoral fisticuffs,
it is a war most still don't understand,
it was the eight thousand kilometres between us,
it was the colour of your toddler skin,
it was fear,
it was me,
it was and still is the inability to see your full face.

This is an ode to a favourite child
using words that can't replace the waning scent of a son.
This is a poem for the guard boat I so wish had found you
    earlier
and for the hope that the captain could be a father.
This poem should absorb every placed blame,
it should place fruit on your grave,
it should refute the two-minute news that cuddled you,
it should be more sorry,
it should give you swimming lessons,
it should take you back to a park with a jungle gym.

This is a stark poem. It is not my place to clean you.
The only intent is presenting your unfathomable beauty,
a three-year-old who could have ridden to moons.

OF COURSE YOU DO FIND SPICY BITS

Today is for an archive.
It is religious and therefore lavish

and habitually cleaned. I've heard
that private libraries and repeat days underground

are the process of book writing
so it's assumed I am poet,

a boy propped over century-
old table in the history

beneath a Montreal summer.
The archivist interrupts

by fingering a mini-canoe reliquary
upon the table between us.

They don't get many visitors.
It is a gift from France. A boat

ferrying brass box no bigger than fist
holds phalanges of Canada's saints

and the finger of Brébeuf angles towards me.
I ignore the angel's gesture, a cliché vestige,

and work to wrench open
a rez school record book.

The Jesuits have been so kind to me.
They've kept meticulous statistics

since day one. There is a purity
in their honesty that is cleansing

or erotic. Makes me nearly
enter the house of solidarity. But instead

I steal knuckles.
.It is difficult to write

with the hands of a saint. I've learned
if you can break a carrot

or fraternity, you too can break
the pointer.

Begin with missionary then proliferate and sprinkle
children over the land. It's as simple as sex on foreign soil,
and the babies will say, "Home. I was born here. Call me
Native too." That's the terror of this ism, I mean the
beauty: if the sights remain short you can't see how you're
weaponized, I mean complicit. Plus, the longer you occupy
a parcel, the easier glory disguises your forebear's faults.

You can call your ancestor's passage an invasion, I mean
an exodus, a historic flight from poverty or famine or
communist murder. Don't worry, the specifics don't
matter; blame fastens poorly to white folx, I mean
European migrants. And take pride in this heritage. Call
it identity, but be sure to vocalize your distance from
the violent and oppressive acts, I mean the harmless
prejudices, even if your insides too boil with the same
arrogant hatred.

Say, "grandma came here alone and with nothing," which
is a lie of course, as she surely wasn't solo aboard that
immigrant boat, and she obviously bore the offspring that
bore you, and she always wore a light skin tone. Remain
ignorant of this. Or at least appear so. Use the phrases
"the good ol' days" and "a different era." And never halt
the infiltration, I mean copulation; infants suggest
innocence but their muscle will build more suburbs.

Remember the keys: blindness and expansion. If you stick to the plan this brilliant strategy will thrive, will make racism, I mean cultural unrest, so legally translucent you can shoot a Cree man in the head, I mean murder, and go unpunished.

NORTHWESTERN

FACING FORT WILLIAM'S ORPHANAGE

Downed grass
where a doe nestled the waist of the Kam
river and car batteries, drowned mattress,
parched condoms, loosestrife;
in the sun, this is where we'll watch.

Gaze on the house-sparrow red
among rail ties rusted below joe-pye,
we're eyeballed by deer ticks,
by bittern around burdock,
by mink in the cattails.

Under cables stitching the sky
we'll number crows in white birch,
count Safeway bags surrendering
near a vulture nest of babies waking.

Daisies ignore a milk jug,
lone mosquitoes probe,
winds persuade pines to recline,
and an airplane sinks beyond the brick carcass
of a brickworks.

Across the river was the school, now ash,
missing children, loitering lavender,
a solar field power-yellow,
and a foundation full of tamarack.

We'll drop prayers by the riverbank,
dredge the waters with our eyes,
lose flakes of spirit by the ripple
and cry amidst the black
of raven screech.

It was time and the thruway loose pack to Slate Falls
that forsook us hours back. Now we exist only as
twenty-two and cockapoo reminiscing down logging road
with me bush-wacked and knapsacked flushing pheasants.
And deep in the dusk of this autumn backcountry
tread two kokums giggling in a pickup. "Have you seen
the white ones?" they ask, with a finger to trees.
The elders are here to forage scrolls, for a tutelage
deciduous and crusty with answers. In so many words
they ask for a meadow walled by granite, a level land
so to ease an arthritic waddle towards bark, towards
strips so ripe one need only to pluck, to release,
paper dropped to feather
down into a black pitch basket.

"Have you seen the white ones?" As settler
I cannot mistake the forest. We stand
in the most flammable woodland, the crisp nobility
of birch a phalanx. But something here I surely missed.
I know because my response to their question is wrong
and paltry and my gut turns when I suggest they
harvest the bark already obviously fallen,
because I require a pencil to reflect
on the enigmatic, because I'm not a speaker
in the language of marcescence laughing around the brush.

SPORE PRINTS

It wasn't known
that the smell of northern forest
could be bagged
and brought home
in a bucket of plucked mushrooms.
Until she did it.

Fungi on the kitchen table
will be sporadically sacrificed
to the art gods.
Are all gods art gods?
Like silk screen,
the meaty gills under caps
will press, will paint
with nature's weight
upon canvas upon canvas.

PROBABLE CAUSE MISJUDGMENT
OF ALTITUDE

Canso or Catalina, like songs of troubadours, time has
brought entombment. This is unearthed in a Google search
and from the tail of c-gffj I find bobbing in Jackson Lake.
It is a grave sight, Consolidated metal in decay
among the shoreline shrubbery.

DHC Beavers gnaw open my day and I find myself
deep online in a nineties thread on the Flying Fireman,
once the world's largest waterbombing outfit, until
a body caught in ready limbs of conifers,
search and rescue photos of a crash into afterlife. Is this end

the *envoi*? A once young crew chief argues for and against,
typing that "a skimmer crusade should always
have an amphib-dog overhead, but when it comes
to the speed of your Noorduyn Norsemen, little matters
but the roar and the ripples."
With no control of wings, I can't help

but agree. Before takeoff, a weathered ranger
fire fighter boy beside me on a Bearskin flight to Thunder
Bay tells how an August morning Airspray bomber
missed the target and dropped one thousand gallons
on him and crew, "raptor sheets of water ripping

half the trees down around me, trunks
like coffins we jumped behind popping
at the peregrine arrival of eight thousand pounds.
Nobody died that time, thank god. Just Jerry
in Red Lake a month before.

Did you ever hear the story of the Flying Firemen
at Y G Q in the Hutchinson Lake cabins,
summer of eighty-two? Stu Wood
had a handgun battle with Charles Ellsworth.
Chuck used a bunk as shield as Stu put six shots
into wall and mattress. I assume both then retired

from holey rooms for a smoke-plumed night
of scotch and sky gazing, nav-lights
festooned between moon and horizon."
When I smalltalk the ghosts of old Metroliners,
I must remember to take preliminary bearings, begin
with an *exordium*, prod passengers for tangibility,
and keep the rhymes consistent. I reply

that Jackson Lake surrendered only spectres
in bomber jackets jabbering lyrics on plane wreck etiquette.
Their word is that scavenging should be prohibited unless
your father or lover died within it
or you were the one killed.

HOW TO PLUCK PHEASANT

Pheasant is colloquial for grouse
and no one has the patience to pluck either.
Plenty of hunters pin boots atop wings,
pull the feet skyward,
breast them out slapdash
and get on with the day.
But this is lazy and wasteful and
makes a barbarous rip.
More time is worth taking, more
attention, a better grip.

Start where the scales of calf meet thigh.
Lift leg feathers and bite
until you gnaw bone.
Place a soft hand on the neck and twirl
until body and mind
disconnect. Snip the wings.
Grab a fist of plumage
like hair of a lover. As you tug,
every fluffy fleece of insulation will fall
to the needle floor.

Pink and skinless, it's time to steal hearts.
Cup the guts and piano your fingers.
Weigh organs until you reach
the chamber below a wind pipe. Pull it
and every piping inside out from the pocket.
Your heaviest thought
will be the gizzard. Cut it

around like an avocado,
never past the pit. Peel
muscle away. If you're in too deep,
a salad of pebbles will spoil the moment.

Garland the nearest tree with innards.
The ravens live for this decoration.
Use fingernails to rake
the cherry puree from abdomen.
The residue from a thousand
mountain ash berries
beds the cavities between ribs.
With water from a freezing creek, feed
the local fish with
what scraps will rinse free. Repeat
with remaining birds.

Use soap. Just kidding. Use a boulder waist-high as a
butcher table. Lay the fish sidelong, backbone across your
belly. Lift the pectoral flipper like a strawberry sepal and
saw beneath the gills until you feel the knife skid upon
the stem. Tilt your head to find the lateral lines. They'll
run parallel to the fissure of quartz in your igneous
cutting board. Use no more than the knife point to nick
the threads stitching the back to the spiny fin. Untied, the
muscle will bulge like you've cut into a couch cushion.
When your slit reaches the soft dorsal, notice the genitals
hiding below. Skewer straight through until the bolster
encumbers the thrust of your stab. The orifice should now
be exposed. Dance your steel along the tailbones into the
wee hours of thin flesh, but don't let the edge split loose
into the morning. Withdraw it secretly, leaving the tail end
coupled and guessing. Return to the head. Run your blade
within the long cut, and the fish will begin to blossom.
Run it again and you'll hear the blunted xylophone of
ribs. Continue this quiet laceration with every small stroke
playing a tune until the music's over. The skeleton of
cuisine should have shimmied into the party. Grind your
heel through the floorboards of belly until the meat has
lost inhibitions and only one clasp of scales is left.
Clutching like a child afraid to get lost, the caudal clings
to the fillet. And like a good parent, don't sever the bond.
Use the vigour as a crutch and flip the skin side down,
opening the fish like a book. Grab the bulk with an honest
hand, slip the blade into that unfolded hinge, and slide
low and slow, scraping against the white mortar of scales

until the opaque gem you've been whittling tumbles free. Time for the Y-bones. If you've brought your tweezers you can pluck the belt like an old picket fence of slivers. If not, finger their outline, then carve until the contour of an earthworm puzzles up from the slab. To finish, remove the smile. The cheeks are a delicacy. Use the flex of your steel to hook a crescent moon out from behind the eye. The hemisphere will flop open like a half cut grape. Pin the skin with your spine, pinch the fruit between thumb and pointer, and pull towards lips until you are juggling the freshwater lucky dollar from palm to palm. Now let's do the other side.

Latch your trail to the tail of a bear.
Notice the blue calm, skies verdigris, a cloud
marmoreal. Notice when the pads of your feet
catch fire. This is the sweet spot.
You have arrived in the bustle of a
lakeless beach. This clearing of shrubs
will surround you. Your kneecaps
will already be blue. Now double over
with your ice-cream pail
until skeeters are a pain in your ass.
It will be August, and beneath the bush
will be a cow's teat. Tweak it
until every berry in the cluster
tumbles into your milk.

Keep an eye up for the bear
or a pack of rogue kokums.
Both are vicious pickers that will purge you
and the blue from an acre in an afternoon.
You will oppose this alacritous harvest
with lassitude. It will now be September.
A blue suppuration will be boiling your wounds.
You will thirst like you haven't watered
for months. The only drink will exist in a
blue capsule. Vertiginous,
your boot will trip or your fingers will slip
and the half-full bucket will topple,
all of your collection pouring
to the ground like deer droppings.

Contrition will crush you, but stay your
hands from panicking a blue retrieval.
The boreal dirt contains blasto.
The berries now wear a dust.
You must rise up and escape
on foot with only what blue you can handle.

TODAY THE TWELVE GAUGE

She rendered the ruffed grouse
undone, burst
by the twelve gauge.

When a chicken dies
its wings drum,
talons capering
ceremonial farewells
before celestial pecking ground.

A number-six shell
took the top half
down with dusk and lead,
hewn portions of bird
plinkoing
through cracks
of spruce.

She disavowed
the needle floor
foul, mortified
at the inclement beat.

THE FOX

Orange against hoared rock
is a fox despairing.
This dormant form
bears pelt
as twofold house and bed.

A question mark of curl,
we spot her from the middle-
class comfort
of our Saturday suv
and subtly discuss
her expiration date
until she squirms away from death.

So I toss her a partridge
from my back seat,
from my humane suffering for life,
expecting the pain calibrating her flattened face
to be relieved with meat,

but knowing in my burning gut
        and her in hers
that this will only delay
the rigorous inevitable
slow sink
of mortality in the moss
and the convocation
of scavenging eagles.

IN THE LEAST DESIRED CORNER

*Every happy man should have some one with a little hammer
at his door to knock and remind him that there are unhappy
people, and that, however happy he may be, life will sooner
or later show its claws*
Anton Chekhov

To live as dis-life,
talons ungrounded
in non-soil, bear becomes
bloat bulged in worst form
of un-health, marbled eyes
like pre-dead rez dog,
nose post-burnt pink, growls
of grated throat, gruff
phlegm panting in chest,
ribs ratcheting down
under only option trans fats.
The bear stares
at death by excess
undernourishment. But there is protest
in grey eyes. This black bulk
guards gravel road, charges
the introspection toll
and marches protest
blockade, canines striking fear
to jam pickups. His hoarse
half-bellow a scream to end inhumane
human years of dumping ruin
into bush, under the inevitable
home of skin, onto
shoulders poked bare.

HOW TO MAKE A SKULL FROM THE HEAD OF A BEAR DELIVERED TUESDAY IN A GROCERY BAG TO THE AFTERNOON OFFICE MEETING

Let it thaw
on a tree stump.
Help the scalp and fur
from bone
with a paring knife.
Evict the eyeballs
with your fingers
like seeds from a pumpkin.
Rest the jaw and
face flesh
atop an ant hill.
Now wait.

Let's work our way down a channel. I'll show you every
elbow and anvil and eddy until we open unto the helix,
the symbol of ear work. But we can't flush this out
without remembering this is a body, and the ear is
employed by the offices of anguished insides, a cavity
with more knots than could ever be untangled. The
corner-room ruler here has always been the prick, so after
years with ear overworked as the only trained listener,
a meeting was called. She pleaded to the prick to double
the staff, explained in her quiet way that more fingers
would not build the answer, that it is ears that are best
at untying knots. But the prick did not listen. Its tiny hole
was not good for hearing, and it always felt the tug of
the old everyday friendship with fingers, a short-sighted
pat on the back kind of rapport that built each other up
more than solved any problems. Plus the fingers were
skilled on the abacus and the foreign toy entertained the
prick beyond proportion, the toy a trick of hypnosis that
deceived viewers into accepting its lack of action. The
beads actually tangled the rope, tied up what could have
been simple solutions, and were incapable of listening.
And so the ear, feeling futility fog the room, recapped with
evidence the potential of aural attention, the assurance
it can develop within demeanour, even if examples of
slack rope remained minimal. The ear even tabled stats on
the pain that fingers and math can cause a vulnerable teen,
and explained that from ears arrives hope which is known
in the north as the central medicine needed for untangling,
and that hope is rarely found in calculators. So here we

are ending this story without words for the climax,
the ear candled but uncleared, and us remembering all the
examples of pricks like this and knowing the infuriatingly
slow time it takes for bodies to grow new parts or discard
old ones with shortcomings. But we can always refer back
to the title.

THE BOREAL

When you have nothing more to text or say
just drive past runways, up old northern roads
that may never end, but steadily erode
until gravel scatters at Pickle Lake.

Expect not to arrive, your journey bewild-
ered by trees adjusting for every tour,
leaves swivelling colours for warblers' allure,
gullies with birch bark lounging in piles

until dusk, when in shield a vein of quartz
blinks, and black crags unlock moose to wallow
roadside and cast eyes down on you. It's now
you'll feel the forest's threat, want to cut short

your trek, but don't worry, slow the drive home,
for fear and darkness ease landscape, like thought,
to one lamplit line: the weaver of knots
is us; the only rule of bush is roam.

I found your porn magazines. They are where you left
them above the giant iron wheels of the abandoned train
coach beside Heritage Park. I didn't mean to invade your
slice of the Kam, and I felt embarrassed that I didn't know
this was a home. Shamefully, the words *crack den* fluttered
through my lexicon, but I never uttered them aloud.
I know addiction too. I left the flavour rainbow of used
condoms on the dirt foyer where you dumped them, and
don't worry, I never dialled municipal cleanup staff for
help. Park janitors are too pernickety for the outdoor-
living flow you have obviously achieved. And I found
hundreds of your needles in the garden's long grass,
orange caps like flowers on a prickly patch of weeds,
infectious stems pointing up to one of the lords above,
and I was instantly aware of how thin my soles are. What
kind of shoes are you wearing? What will you plant when
summer eventually arrives? Just so you know, I wasn't
here long. I was worried you'd return while I was in, label
me a b&e assailant of outdoor dwellings (if that's a thing),
or label me a cop (I certainly don't appear a poet), or
maybe you'd think I too was expecting sex. Thankfully,
nothing happened. And I left your magazines on the shelf.
I'll pop by tomorrow just to check in, see how you're
doing. Maybe bring the pooch by for a visit. But I'm
ashamed I don't know how a home like this works. When
I arrive, do I knock at some place of entrance? I don't
want to overstep if you need the space. You're obviously
been through some stuff lately. Obviously still going
through it.

VALHALLA

A book advises I bet heavy tonight,
so I gamble on northern bingo halls,
kick the doors open, erupt into paradise.

The afterlife is rich with one-legged
locals stumping Labatt's, hospital tenants
wheeling carrion, bannock at the grand buffet.

My guardian winks within white dress,
jingles her carillon, coyly pats an empty seat,
then fondles my slacks to snip surviving twenties.

Past isle of flashing mountains,
bells and whistles signal bonus lives bestowed upon
a bonspiel of arthritic honky-tonk grannies.

They blab that the trick to winning remains
honourability, Sorels, and an abundance
of gold and walleye heaped upon your pyre.

THIS ISN'T ABOUT ME OR A TITLE

I elect to use the minds that shaped me,
Amartya's and Lee's and Dionne's,

to again draw the concomitant dots
between race and death, to evade the vehemence

of open social combat, of news media
so short and partial it increases murder rates,

of poetry's hackneyed political clichés.
But don't think that in my creative evasion

of these venomous distractions
I am blind to what's happening on the streets.

And when I write *what's happening*
I mean Phillip squaring the Ron's obtuse electoral riggings,

I mean Whitney now "missing" in T-Bay,
I mean the digital infection of racist death threats.

And when I type *streets*
I mean the buses on Dundas East and West,

I mean the YouTube comments,
I mean Cat Lake.

SIOUX LOOKOUT

This model is the future of healing, a racialized maker movement, a walk-in-welcome 3D printing playhouse where Leonel Lac Seul untangles his past in CAD and designs an object that slices his drinking in half by layering 0.3 mm of potential in every pass. Trellised with tech, our small-town print farm can cure more illness than a needle. We offer a space of respite unlike a medical clinic, a space that can ignore the breath of morning Kelly's if your fingers can still feed the polylactide plastic strings of a memory into the teeth above an extruder. It's for this reason that Leonel arrives to guide dreams into a PTFE tube, to transform a social assumption by letting Bondtech gears grind his thought then spit it through a pinhead hotend at 215°C until every layer of the picture has been reformed with a third dimension. This version of health seeks contagion, requires 1 kg spools of filament, converts .stl files to .gcodes, and can be built with any colour of turmoil. Here you'll find the specs for success and see the material it takes to turn hope tangible, flauntable, pocketable for use some later day. This model leaves no overhangs without a scaffold, no bed without a raft.

I am boy, your jeering tongue dubbing me
Evan Almighty because I appear weekly
with all the whitest toys for learning
and I challenge local kindness by offering myself
freely and unceasing
and void of racist caveats.

I am boy, futile for problem solving,
my ear powerless but open
to hear your Christmas story
of being kidnapped
then locked up five days
in a shit-smelling Hudson bedroom.

I am boy, maamaakaac wemihtikooshi,
amazing whiteman because I don't steal
your children or stories like Tikinagan
or Liberals, but I'll bring the filament
to 3 D print a Wendigo, and I'll shut
up and listen if you're explaining it.

Gala oxfords sidestepping pedestrians
like I'm clambering deadfall
in Sioux bush hunting
a lunch meeting like spruce grouse
under limbs at the end of logging road.

With nothing but cement
squaring the Sheraton, I find myself
chin-wagging the anthropologist
panhandlers actively mapping
the networks of attitude,
of game trails, of voles
escaping collared coyotes
into the brush of a fresh limed
brick wall.

            Blaze orange
would bring safety to my demeanour
for all the same reasons as
up north. The vest would scream:
this flesh is meant for eyes and teeth;
do not rip my skin
with bullets; I am one
with fire, but do not lose me
in the rush hour of a thicket.

HOW TO STAY ALIVE ON THE STREETS
OF SIOUX LOOKOUT

In the summer, preserve a water bottle.
Know the places with a public phone.
Regularly call your mother and council.
For lunch there is soup at the shelter.
Remember a private place to take a shit.
Learn how to hide liquor inside a coat.
In the winter, drink less Kelly's.
In a pinch, warm in a bank lobby.
If life gets tough, drink more Kelly's.
The hospital is a last resort.
Empties are worth money.
Remember who can access a We Card.
Keep a distance from most white folx.
Finish dirty jokes in Oji-Cree.
Keep your feet moving when the OPP patrol.
The Kenora Jail is worse than cold or hunger.
The shelter is not always welcoming.
Be wary of drinking with unknown faces.
Don't invite new folx to your camp.
Find a lover to watch your back, and for other stuff ...
Never let the campfire go out.
Always keep your clothes dry.
Always give to those in need.
Keep an eye on the crows. They are smart and silly.

A KINGFISHER NAMED BEAR

for Sol Mamakwa

He stands in the Park
of a Queen who tries to kill him.
They expect him to sing a song
that orders a foreign god to save her.
They expect him to sing the song
of a Politics that accepts the annexation of land.
They expect him to avoid a dialect
cuz none have learned the tongue flip
that honours water over leadership.
He stands in the chamber and again
explains he will only square to
a labour strike or a pipeline fight
when his children stop dying
and the water returns.
They expect him to smile.

Lace little fingers
fashioning wedding dress
with white filament
from 3 D printing pen
within our library.
The teen is all silence,
all colours of hair,
hands steady designing
chiffon in minuscule
in a contest with younger sister.

Filament is lactic acid,
is polyester corn,
so the figurine gown
is one part carcinogen,
one part native land.
This is future fashion,
and the teen is Oji-Cree,
is undersized,
is smiling,
is racialized,
is talented,
is androgynous –
this turning into one's self –
and they have all the tools
to layer future,
to see the shimmer,
to smell the shame
of plastic and culture
and marriage from every gendered angle.

My workshop ends
before a head is deposited
on butterfly sleeves.
Like sediment,
this story is built
from ground up,
is made of downfall,
is accumulating
like every great art,
is unfinished.

Today you are the man before me paying for groceries.
The man Monday smiling from within a familial clique,
a mother, a lover, a handful of children. But last week you
were the man in black on black with black cap and face
tat, the man entering my office wobbly and demanding
turn at the public phone, the man I saw selling smack
out back, the man asking our receptionist to sit sexy on
his lap, the man soon to escalate a threat. Your old friend
Thomas told me you are a gang man, a man who as
toddler was forced to drink a bottle harder than milk, a
man once moulded by the knuckling demands of a father,
a man taught too early how to cull an excess of puppies,
a man untaught how to whisper, a man whose father died
and left him believing that violence is a synonym for love,
a man who found food and comradery with a leadership
of likeminded victims, a gang man.

Yesterday you screamed at me, shattering the decorum
of our office foyer. When an attack taunted in your every
curse, when your uproar peaked and you slowed, raised
your chin, and cocked hands behind your back, when
your nerves from this climax shuddered your shoulders,
when your face burst with every obvious turn of your
mind's wheel, every desire to fuck this white dude up
and snap in half the phone already on with the OPP, when
your thoughts tumbled their way through the timelines of
atonement, when this electric moment crackled, it was the
absence of fear that most frightened me. You were silent
and glowed euphoric in this pulsive moment, and my

insides were static, no adrenaline pumping a rescue, no flight, no fight. And in the excited screens of your eyes I watched every other tragedy from my slides of other office days, all my first aid first responses, all the emotions that mistook me for counsellor, all the hands lost in cuffs. This moment layered until all the pictures of blood and Kelly's and tears smothered the light.

Today I hurry from the market to a dentist but find I'm thirty minutes too early. I'm forced to sit pondering the dynamics between your face once a calm dynamite and the one that moments ago didn't notice me. This only ends when a waiting-room courtesy TV flickers a feature film on a desert war effort. A khaki-camo field doctor stumbles into frame and into metaphors: "Conflict-induced adrenaline is like cold water. These warrior boys out here, they've been thrown into the pool so many times that eventually they start to enjoy it, start jumping in all by themselves. And then there are others, some of the corpsmen, that are forced to work so many days in the water, they just lose their sense of temperature. Either way, the body ain't meant to be that cold that often."

Amy has a new haircut because her baby died.
It happened two days ago.

Last month, we ironed the baby's name across a T-shirt,
Everley Grace Rose, pink and bold
so the baby could read it when born.

Last week, Amy stopped in to use the public phone
and I had to tell her she was bleeding on the common chair.
When I left work that day, my eyes found the chair
legs up inside the dumpster.

Amy tells me the haircut is a rally
and the bright new colours speak to her,
but I struggle to hear anything past her stumbling gait
and the sobering stench of Kelly's
and my shock at the numbness we've both forced to the
    surface.

The ways we try to fix ourselves.
The things discarded.

DERMIS TO GOLD

for Amy Morris, 1988–2019

Ambling through our April door dressed toque to toes in
pink, every second a succession of bright ideas on how to
force Spring's arrival by expression of self in colour. With
this exploit of spring we work and learn along the days,
creative apparel always the aim, always labelling family
names, children's slang, Big Trout home logos. You steady
the tremors of withdrawal, glisten into the skills of a
hands-on future, a hand ambitious, an artisan in bloom.
But you also meet the spectres of past, watch your dermis
slurring to gold, so we speed-print each treasure on
a T-shirt in too short a time, hustle against the clap
of synapse cracking like the May breakup between
the thawing ice roads of your insides and the islands
of progress around us.

When I revisit this mortality, it argues I should have
helped more, that if our lessons flowed beyond the steep
banks of my nine-to-five, you would have had a flooded
forest of learning to wade within, a rich replenishment of
ideas to carry you through the evenings, to naturally soak
your mind and free time, to paddle you past an alcoholic
boredom. What I'm saying is, I remember walking past
you beside the grocery store on a cool May evening. You
were one in a huddle of black hoodies, and all I gave was
a hollow grin from the corner of my brisk and unvaried
stride.

Afloat on the June powwow grass, I spot your hospital
wheelchair opposite a canoe teeming with cartons of fruit
juice, iced tea, bottled water. You lived alone in that
moment with no one to push you through the lineup of
your last days, wheel you under the tent for a free plate
of fried fish. And I just stood there, lethargic opposite that
juice-filled canoe, no harmless hello, no flattery offered
on the font choice of your coral sweater, no nerve to look
past the bold yellow monster stealing the tinge from
your cheeks.

Today it takes me four tries to thread my fishing line
through the loop on my leader. I'm alone on a lake near
the north highway, and it's clear from my hands that I've
not come to grips with your loss. This could never be a
eulogy because I left the edge of class between us. You
were reduced to a work friend, your troubles my task
of employment, your death a new note on my calendar.
I know these reactions were wrong and I owe you a
proper vignette. But to sketch I must reopen your coffin,
which I still lack the courage to do. The pain I still need
to elude, so I withdraw into this August bush and fish,
cast this casket image into Vermilion River because
I remain too frightened to grieve you.

EVEN IF THE CHILD'S LOST, MOTHERS NEVER LOSE THE TITLE

Night wind wraths
like autumn spirit mad

at boy's body ruined
by a liquor, then

by a train, Tuesday
after midnight

in a rail yard two blocks away.
What is often forgotten

is that the spirit
of greatest window-pane clatter

is the live one
of a mother

grieving beneath lamplight
on a station landing

north of tracks.
The anguish in exhales

whistling the taunt
to step forward

into traffic
or back.

IT'S NO REAL PLEASURE IN LIFE
OR, HOW TO VIEW THE KIDS AT NIGHT

A gathering of teenagers, a bundle of fifteeners
in a trash-infested valley past the snowbank,
they are ahoot, howling, smashing
and some have begun dying in ice-
bergs of vodka beside the rail line,

and the kids are drowned
by locomotion, a train cutting onward
all night, like every night,
along a track stitching forest,

and a conductor ignores, gazing
beyond his boxcar herd he sees only
twinkly lights pulsing on a short row of homes,
beautiful houses all Christmas cared-for,
woodland homes hillcrest reclining,

homes that could bed tonight's expiring children,
homes with folx who could and should care more,
and above all, northern stars the eyes of a critic
never turning face the other way.

BEAR PAW AND BEAST

for Paul Mahoney, 1980–2019

In death your liver was flint, amber rock embedded, beast
sacrificed for horns and broken yoke. I want to unearth,

spit, rub clean, brandish near steel, ignite a fire,
memorialize. You, ahead of death, possessed pride,
enterprise, a rebuilt powerhouse of self. I doubt the uses
of *success* but I still rest the word upon your name.

At the viewing, a father wept through confessions. Your
union with booze once sanctified by family. Those were
party days, myopic days, a bottle of beer on a preteen
birthday

always, the first drink as rite. Winter nights by water
tower, you erected camps, lodged warm with whiskey.
Bonfire fights and love making your body. Pupils like
dusk,

engorged they bred in every repeat northern town
you bounced to. Now restless sovereign children, packs
of future ancestors joust and shout in this sticky house-
of-worship funeral service.

Brawn was your bear paw prison tat. Let it trail a
trackable path after death, plug claws into the lichen
and begin regrowth.

HOW TO WRITE A POEM ABOUT
DEAD CHILDREN

Some poems can live without souls
but mine remain ghastly fools flicking
uncomfortable narratives like
cigarette butts during class change.
I'd benefit from better line breaks but
shards of hard truth already hazard
my corners, pebbles of politics at ankle height
tripping the feet.

I'm still learning how to write
poems about dead children. It's unclear
if words should cling to memories
or dirt. Maybe it's better to lay
entire undertakings bare,
casket open, and cradle the body
while the town shovels soil over us.
Maybe it's better if we crack
the ceremony with a scream.

So much of a child's smile implies
that this encasing earth is unsettled.
To fidget in discomfort is to worm
and is repugnant and is as nature.
Once I called this book a morgue
but you might say we're past that.
We'd all prefer this pain and poem
to not exist
but.

BARBLESS

And the dead simply
don't stumble indoors again.
And this unhappening happens
vacantly, meaning wordless,
or vacationally, like she's just hitched
a ride off to Winnipeg.
Then these two vacuums conspire
to nurture a norm in the workspace
void of emotional harm.

And when someone dies
to whom I committed just less than friendship,
I nudge the status down
to acquaintance
and avoid the barb.
Now nothing hooks to the heart
on the way out.

And nothing around me shifts:
again the colleagues joke-bicker
about coffee brewing strength,
and the bylaw truck tickets
remain racially fragrant,
and the livers of half the north
continue to melt,
and a handful of our students
vanish by this grave organ,
and our fledgling MP
debates gun control,
and the aspens don't shiver
because it is a still day.

Have you ever seen lips so bulged and thick from frost that
you beg for them to burst? Michael speaks to me between these,
sips soup within these. Mike is a man so close to home,
only one flight from a mother in Deer Lake, but day upon
day the plane leaves without him, and night upon night he
absconds from my aid and waddles bum-kneed, hobbles
to locked-bank lobbies, creeps circles for warmth within
fluorescent foyers, acts as illegal ATM concierge while the
air around him drops lower and slower and grinds closer
to a killing coldness. Mike, he is a survivor, and if lucky
around midnight he will sleep rough and alive beneath a
totem of capital failures, a hungry homeless head on cement
just inches from banknote pillars, the pillows of green queens.

Daily I find feet twined in the sky, Mike snared and
pendulumming upside down in deep love, mind hooked
to a crowd tumbling around LCBOS and bush fires, heart
hooked to a woman, gut hooked to the promise of
afternoon soup. He admits he'd fly away if he wasn't
tethered, if he could talk his stomach and knees into the
gamble. But Mike knows our airport, only three kilometres
north, in this weather, with his poor leg, it is a walk to a
frozen end, a flurry burial in a ditch. I learn all this while
holding the spoon, Mike's fingers too bitten by winter to
bend, his tears collecting in the bowl on his lap. His lips say
the tears are made of a longing for home, made of moans
from survival without a mattress, made of cries for a
mother. His lips say he is most frightened by his own
ominous turn towards tolerance of death's nightly
harassments.

NONE HAVE BLED ON THESE STREETS
MORE THAN JIM

Broken mirror has no need to slice
human skin. There is no rule
of laceration. When I find Jim's head
plugging the asterisk in entrance-door glass,
there are no teeth in his artery.
No breach. And his first request
is to accept his apology, the second
to hurry him free for the urinal.

It's guaranteed when assisting Jim
for blood to surface from kneecap, from knuckle,
from nose or other orifice. His vertigo
leads to head injuries, leads to drinking,
leads to tumbles (read this line any direction
and the sequence still fails). But today
is for the fortunate. The levees of skin
and Carhartt collars hold.

The medics mistrust my claim
of finding such modest human leakage.
They find the carotid persistence odd
and a stumble expected of elderhood. This ignominy
is wrong. And while escalation to wreck-
age is rite, for Jim the most violent
reflection is urinary. Nothing cuts
away dignity like piss in a trouser.

Today we play by a rule
and banish Savannah from
the Learning Centre, from her daytime home,
because two weeks back
we saw her punch a friend
in the head, then in the breast
because the friend said
Savannah should not be drunk
while pregnant four months
with twins.

And as I leave work today,
Savannah's sprawled asleep on the steps outside.
I thank gods it is summer
but question the righteousness
underwriting our office policy.
We define a culprit,
inflict a border of verbs,
scatter the title of victim,
abandon her to the sun,
multiply the boilers,
restrict the water,
and claim all in the name of safety.

From my bag I grab a mistreated two-pack of cookies
and slip them beneath the broken zippers
of Savannah's knapsack.
But the equation of the day still fails.
Our protocol for expulsion crumbles
when divided by all the rips in her backpack
and the emptiness of two extra bellies.

MY PROSE POEM FROM INSIDE
THE PRECINCT

When you know the name of every grocery-store shopper,
a CBC story attached to your town creates a texture in the
skin of conceit and resentment. You're both proud and
pained. The article presents a popular death, and by
popular I mean mainstreet sidewalk public with many
witnesses, friends of the deceased with heavy tears and
digestible adjectives. And by popular I mean violence non-
domestic and with loads of gore, violence a quiet step
too far from the stale phrase *generational trauma*. The
reporter brands a man as "killer" but his real name is
Felix. They hint at *gang member* but leave void a
backstory. They highlight his fresh release from prison,
but dance around the word *race*. It's hard to prove
poverty, hard to point a finger at the newspaper's funder.
But we need not worry. The fruit between the lines hangs
low and is ripe for plucking. The truth is evident in what
is left unsaid. Unsaid how medias prowl for vicious news,
the more pain the more bucks from suburban blood-boner
addicts. Unsaid that the only time this town sees a CBC
SUV is when a clean-cut murder occurs. Unsaid how a
government's chronic underfunding left Felix the "killer"
once a kid alone with no counsellor, that without local
medics the gang was the next up with medicine. Unsaid
that when so many decades of pain occur, a gang can offer
a bonfire of hope, food over tummy grumbles, drugs over
pain, action over stasis. Unsaid that posting only one
constable for community policing is a pitiful approach to
gang enrolment prevention. Unsaid why we only punish
the end face, the Indigenous face, of broken colonial

justice logic. Unsaid that Felix is the son of a deadbeat
Parliament stepfather and a layabout Justice stepmom.
Unsaid that this should be a public shame. Unsaid that
if pushed to hunger's death edge you too would kill your
way out. And if it sounds like I'm defending a killer,
I am not. I'm just slipping in here after dark to swap
the mugshot with one of a minister.

Someone should write homage to you in verse,
expand your memorial beyond a poem dedication,
magnify your memory until the high school's tragic
annual statistic is just a footnote. But this cannot be my job,
as I was two degrees your stranger,

and the flowers that were your life are now wrapped
in red tape, a bouquet tied by the ribbons of privacy,
and it is not my place to cut your stories loose. But the gust
of your loss still feathers your petals to my ear
and I assemble the foliage into an image

audacious like the local blacksmith boy
who wrought a backyard garage into career
before grade twelve grad, the boy forging a future
sharp and endurable as his Damascus blades,

slick like the witty bars of the hip-hop boy
in the Gay-Straight Alliance studio beneath the MP's office,
his warrior rhymes marching up stairs with demands
of emancipation from the oppression overhead,

green like the hair tips of the videographer boy budding
to life in tech room nights, a popcorn-dinner architect
    cutting
the crap from TV on a library laptop, twiddling
the shared ukulele to cheer up a retina break with peers.

And nothing I've just written contains your life,
as I know too little to sketch a portrait.
But the vibrant palette above surely contains your inks,
the energy, the truth, the youth,
and with these I paint the shades of a garden
and we know you stand somewhere within it.

There are many families like the Chapmans, many with a
mother's eyes ablaze with wisdom, hands clapping flour in
the sun for baking on a spring day, hunger alit by children
grubby-faced and gorgeous, a toddler's hair an inferno,
the munchkins sweaty from the skip gallop return from
every schoolday. The loss of this family overnight is
synonymous with *house fire*, with a quick ten-minute burn
of kin into cinder, with a second-hand pain that can
smother you.

In a small northern town, it is one thing to watch smoke
snake towards the clouds and another to remember the
humans in its embers. This is the unlabelled step beyond
traumatic. And hot on its smouldering heels is the prelude
to healing, a job for an optimist, someone tender but
armoured. They must choose what charcoal was
particleboard and what was once half-grown human.
They must knead the grief from hands that hold the
sorting shovel in the grave frame of aftermath. They must
rinse the dust from a neighbourhood's linens before it
settles into depressions. They must be willing to light the
next fire.

In the Ornge fixed-wing is Larissa sitting for seventy
rattling minutes in paramedic thought. She will unbuckle
in the imminent aftermath of when a building in
Kitchenuhmaykoosib Inninuwug was blackened like a
battleground. What gauze do you bring to bandage the
wounds of burn victims already dead? If the fire

extinguished hours ago, when is the emergency over?
After her airborne ambulance lands, a pickup truck drops
her at the Big Trout ashes to help a man from the nest he's
made beside the coals, a man with a father's prudence
now crawling behind his eyes, a man with fingers
evaporated by flame, a man outbursting hysteric with a
near-vegetable mind. He comments on the impotence
of words.

Days later, I find a man crouched in a Sioux Lookout
nook drinking wine beside my office door. I begin our chat
with an attempt to console, and his growls say that I can't,
and his shout says that he'll take his toddlers' bodies
home himself tonight. He is cradling a shrivelled onion,
says he found it live, surviving in the air ducts, says his
lack of tears belittles him so he's heaving them artificially,
says I am a feeble listener, says that the crackle from the
onion peel should make me think the house is still on fire,
because it is.

Sky jaundice,
a yellow that out-fogs a sun
like solstice responded
to our friend dead this week,
a sympathy solace
cautious with colours,
cautious like me with the turmoil
creasing a workday smile,
cautious like colleagues' words
when declaring a way that she died.

This week's failure of a friend to heal
makes unreal every atmosphere,
makes smoky plumes unavoidable
and I am smothered,
my unappeasable insides
sick of broken health services,
policy measured apology narratives,
my insides sick from the charcoal
feathering down as ochre mist.

Yellow
like how her liver's fight
stained her once-white sclera.
Yellow like filleted walleye
once I've mistakenly nicked the gall.
Yellow like Pantone 130 C
painted on her hospital room walls.
Yellow like iodine
spilt in her palliative wing.
Yellow like politics
or the blemish of apocalypse.

You know why town doesn't look so
broken? Streets run methodically, as symbiosis
where toxins enter the homeless
sheltered neatly, no, nightly under our office awning
from October rain, and the eight a.m.
retired man with white grocery bags
discovers pain, no, green festive Kelly's boxes
sprinkled within a rock
garden that protects our vinyl siding
and that rolls drunken ankles. Synergy

is when the old man eyes through my soul,
no, my morning office window and our insight grows
voiceless that every carton means
liver failure, no, ten cents
and we together share
a secret of how the front entrance looks so
unsettling, no, clean
before the MPP arrive.

DYSMORPHIA

Afraid of her ventricles
bloody heart electro pumping
veins visibly echoing tempo
so she never wears tank tops.

Near a nipple ribs raise
smidgen with all impact
like fist inside flicking rhythm
she believes body monster.

They say it is heart of Goliath
she hears "haphazardly" tough
she volunteers to sever slice nerve
lightning engine of humanhood.

She feels the time to escalate
pluck inner bulb problem
like onion from earth
of a fruitful autumn.

We watch her world on a roll
we parent practitioners
see heart hop a bleeding bounce
a trapped rabbit escaping skin.

IN A SMALL NORTHERN TOWN

Is this "positive"?
Marlon Riggs

Let us show you daughter
whose uncle visits after two weeks
at Musselwhite to surprise her, pull her
from Pelican, fly her
back to Sachigo,
and spend six days with rifles
in the bush. To be family
is to kill a moose.

Let us show you cousin,
she's titled King Street Queen,
she has no house for home
but when that vulture of winter lands
she stands with a stick in defence,
persuades friends to drink less,
notes whose toes need fresh socks,
and never lets a campfire extinguish.

Let us show you sister
who's spent a lifetime transitioning
from failure to lawyer,
from boy to femininity.
It's been an epochal adjustment
of small-town tongues and stares
but today the only comment
highlights her empathy in the court.

Let us show you auntie,
she's back at Equay-wuk
again, and that means
she's kicked off the Kelly's
again. And her short poise
remains a totem, see the friends stand
to join this disturbance.

Let me show you niece
who blossomed her first baby
at fifteen like her mother,
and like her mother at fifteen,
and that great-grandma, oh
the smiles at every bingo!
She always speaks of the power
in numbers.

And there is nothing here
no thing to see
no black trans mental health lead
no pushback to toxic trustee policy
no atypical model for vulnerable teens
no option for comradery
no tongue for pronoun they
no schoolboard ruffled by change
no rifts in colonial archetype

nothing wrong anymore
no admin principals this white
no subtle racism ingrained
no queers or gays
no drugs to ease the pain
no lack that makes this town more sore
more sorrowful, more poor.

TO THE BOY POUNDING ON OUR BACK DOOR
AT MIDNIGHT

I cannot let you in. This phrase has undertone. It's
uncomfortable and writhes like the fists tumbling in your
hoodie pouch. It contains venom like the drippings from
your chin to the chest of your September orange sweater.

Your eyes are vexed and I judge there is a high probability
of violence upon self or against others. My insinuations
are staunch and startle me as much as your failure to hide
from my porch light the minority in your damaged face.

I know firsthand how shock can foxtrot a mind. I start
our conversation with empathy and yell an apology
through the hinges. Immediately I feel the rebound, a
reflection of futility cutting with the glow of my light skin,
my foreign Canadian language, and my racism cleverly
masked behind the deadbolt of safety-first.

On the phone, dispatch assures my harmless home is just
another on a strip of hedgerow neighbours who've
encountered you knuckling for nocturnal resolutions
at backdoors. We've all remedied your pain by howling
to police.

At your age, I doubt you can see all of the barriers
between your pleas and my medicine cabinet, so I demand
that you meet me out front in the streetlight, but an officer
finds you wedged between our side stucco wall and the
fence post.

When they finally wrench you free, you're casually escorted to the back seat of a cruiser, no cuffs, no rough stuff. I hear a cop assuring, "there'll be no jail tonight, son. We'll just patch you up and give you a lift home." You respond with the life span of "please don't."

TO THE MAN STABBED LAST WEEK BEHIND
MY BACK FENCE

Police dawdled over from the station kitty-corner
and I confessed, I never see our backlane victims.
Our northern murderers work a loose nine to five, take
    a long lunch,
and Wednesday's killer is likely a friend.
I've had plenty of backyard bonfire evenings,
me leaning in plastic patio chair opposite that chunk
    of alleyway defence,
but I only ever see spectres through my cracking slats.
Night or day the thoroughfare is only stop-motion,
a blurry old film where your eyes don't admit characters
but instead connect flickers, see appendages flinging,
witness a throat exposing howl, a stab motion,
the freeze frames of someone all black being chased,
the rigours of a sprint, kicks of unsettling footfalls flinging
    gravel.

Kids always run back there. I always assume the shadows
    are kids
and then all's simply playful,
not murderous as it could be if I think adults.
The adrenaline's kept down this way. This is a quiet town
and our backyard is our cliché haven, an outdoor family
    playroom.
Out there last week, I used a knife to saw open burger buns,
used a knife to shave bonfire roasting sticks to stabbing
    points,
used my leg as cutting brace and stuck one knife stroke
    too far,

❧

put the sharp end inside a thigh, felt the blade inside cold
like an ice cube forced upon a summer-warm back,
like the smell of Listerine behind a rural library.

Thursday, when I ask about you to the street folx
    warming near my office door,
they simply say you didn't die. They say it was just a little
    knife.

Let us imagine Child, say they're born in a place where staring at feathered friends in the sky is forgotten, a place where too few have been taught how to cope, and so Child, like the wealth of local children, too easily finds a liquid solution. And then Child turns fourteen and they see slivers of a future that they want and deserve so they're shipped down to Sioux with a crew of preteen buddies and boarded in scattered basements with tattered single beds replacing parents. But addiction doesn't end with relocation, and a new town doesn't teach you to cope.

A mother or kokum or auntie of father is now four hundred crow-flights away and none have a cellphone cuz it's never been needed before. But Child still has a handful of buddies, line mates to begin this southern life game together with heads electric and running and never able to sleep. Confusion doesn't summarize the battles Child fights in these first few days. Child's here to educate but quickly they exhaust from new things and no sleep and in fatigue nothing sticks. But somehow the body tingles to make new friends and in so many ways, like at any age, friends and tingles can possess you, can fill you up, fill that sadness chasm inside.

And all of these beautiful friends, they are varieties of Child, all yearning for a northern home, missing touch, missing too much to truly offer anything. And all the medias tell us that it's so easy to fill the missing hole, just grab the drink and allow its hug and kiss to envelop. So, sidestepping the guidance office, Child embraces the hard

stuff every time the final bell rings and the sun goes down.
Of course Child wakes up and the head hurts, but the
mickey gives them a ride back to class and another packs
them a lunch and so the school becomes more their home
than the lonely suffering in this stranger's basement.

The only folx that really care make loud demands in the
classroom, take attendance, grant a motivating A grade,
and push the brain to think beyond brinks. But that
school is all kinds of white and formal, and teachers
today, they smell the alcohol. Today, Child meets the new
man, Trouble, face to face. And from his office, there is
an exit parade, then suspension for days, the hope struck,
a future crushed again. So Child copes like back home
with a bottle for backbone but now more alone and more
growling darkness every day until they question, "Who
would really notice me gone?" Then Child makes plans
and writes notes and every second the world of relatives
sinks into raucous dusk until Child themselves are all that
is left in the dimming. But like a poet thick with edits they
don't notice the days roll

to freedom, to classroom roads reopened. Child hears
wings on fresh air and again gets outside and breathes
and shakes away a few chips of darkness and walks with
no bullshit cuz they're not young and dumb like white
Trouble and his principles said, cuz there's no going back
to that crypt. Child gets to class on time and doesn't drink
before or at lunch, only evenings with a tight crew, just
boys and girls and inbetweens, people who'll watch out
for them cuz they know the struggle, the misery when
apart from the outside world, the despair when knowledge
is blocked, the tears that dry without a mother, the tyrant
in a body that craves booze.

Friends try anything to keep Child smiling: candy, cuddles, movies, even offer a late-night dubbie. They tell Child this is healthy, at least better for your body, so Child tries it and yep, its power is eclipsing. It quiets the intensity of pressure, it slows the day down, and Child asks friends to get more and more until they're living in smoke, rolling a J with the morning Shreddies, puffing a bedtime lung on the pillow. We must remember the pace of time for a teen.

It's after lunch and Child's woken up back-down on a classroom desk, too much weed in the cookies meant for mending the midday stress. It's the intercom again, the lord above calling him to the gates. Child's off to the office again and they say a locker smells like skunk and they jab with lines like "you might be done here." And Child cries with the fear that they'll send them home, a future is crumbling, and even at that incandescent office desk Child is crushed again by the darkness and every angle of the room shrinks and Child feels the chill like a fish hooked from water knowing, this is it. But no, a counsellor arrives with the phrase "don't worry."

They call it empathy, and offer it now to patch the bleeding from this pointed moment. And they take Child next door and leave, and it's just Child and her, a new staff just here to listen, and guess what, the nurse smiles and curses and keeps her ears open and Child quickly erupts, lets it all out because the nurse is real and admits she feels the darkness too and bares the truth that "you'll never be done with night" but she can offer lamps. And after weeks of chatting, Child finds it, sitting beside the bulb is a friend with feathers, hope.

POTTERY, AN IMPOSSIBILITY

The vacancy you're hearing is
anguish missing, and I can't and won't

try to jamb anything into that hole
because I've never lived

a life as Oji-Cree.
It's the disacknowledgment of race,

not just the whiteness, but the skin
so involved in the suffering

and my bullshit mortgage-rate-
retirement-fund distance from it.

And even if I can name the pain
precisely, medically,

remould it blind in clay
from practice handling it every day,

it will always be hollow pottery, an impossibility
blatant in the writing,

clay always obviously stolen,
tone never matching my palms.

Before editing this poem, I called
this idea Theory,

but after a few times around
I've unmasked it as my giant imposter

syndrome, an urban university spectre declaring
Evan has no place here

alongside this issue, no right
to take this space, no right

to write what was handed over in drunken trust
by a bleeding mother.

In this way I go days, dejected weeks
rejecting words until an aging friend

rebuilds me. She does this with
quietude, with creativity

self-centred and infectious.
In our silent crafting I find

humanity. And by humanity I mean
instinct, the humbling, humane drive

to lessen another's suffering,
to add an umpteenth effort to straighten

a crooked democracy,
to exhale

into beads and needle
all that is vicariously burdened upon me,

to exhale, for all my friends,
into a pencil.

NOTE TO READERS

I live in and write from a remote town in Northwestern
Ontario, where the majority of residents are
Anihshininiwag, Oji-Cree people. My daytime
employment involves operating a drop-in adult education
centre used primarily by the local homeless community.
Racism, sexism, ableism, and colonialism are everywhere
in our community. For this reason, I have tried to push my
poems into difficult spaces and expose truths that involve
my relationships with others, including my friends from
more vulnerable communities. As a white, cisgender, male,
able-bodied settler, I recognize that I speak from positions
of privilege that oppress others. My intention is not to
insert false words into anyone's mouth, speak for any
other culture, or disrespect vulnerable bodies around me.
In these poems, I have tried to speak about social
injustices to incite conversation and action.

Huldufólk are Icelandic elves. The folklore of Gimli, a hotspot of Icelandic immigration to Manitoba, maintains that two Huldufólk reside in the old schoolhouse attic.

The term "zebras" refers to zebra mussels. The term "greenback" is an idiom for walleye.

In the most reproduced media photos, Alan wears a red T-shirt emblazoned with the text "Invaders: Mystery Space Riders." Tima Kurdi, Alan's aunt, purchased this shirt for Alan. I am immeasurably grateful to Tima for her book *The Boy on the Beach* (Toronto: Simon and Schuster, 2018).

The title "Of course you do find spicy bits" is a line from James Joyce's story "A Little Cloud."

The final line of "Colonialism for dummies" refers to the murder of Colten Boushie.

Select phrases in "Probable cause misjudgment of altitude" are from the documentary film *Bush Pilot: Reflections on a Canadian Myth*, directed by Bob Lower and Norma Bailey (NFB, 1980).

"In the least desired corner" was written during time at Shoal Lake 39 First Nation. I thank the people of Iskatewizaagegan for allowing me to visit.

Kelly's is an inexpensive brand of fortified wine.

The phrase "maamaakaac wemihtikooshi" means "amazing whiteman" in Oji-Cree and was spoken to me by the elder and language expert Jerry Sawanas.

The title "It's no real pleasure in life" is a line from Flannery O'Connor's story "A Good Man Is Hard to Find."

The title "In a small northern town" and many other lines in this book were birthed from lines in Rosanna Deerchild's book *this is a small northern town* (Winnipeg: Muses' Co., 2008).

Musselwhite is a goldmine, Pelican Falls is a boarding school, and Equay-wuk is a wellness and support program.

ACKNOWLEDGMENTS

Earlier drafts of poems from this book have been published in the *Antigonish Review*, *EVENT*, *subTerrain*, *Contemporary Verse 2*, *Blank Spaces*, the *Literary Review of Canada*, *Bywords*, and *Vallum*. "Bloor-Yonge" won the 2018 Vallum Award for Poetry. "A stab motion, a quiet town," a suite of five poems from this book, was a runner-up for the 2019 Lush Triumphant Literary Award for Poetry. "Colonialism for dummies" was a runner-up in the 2020 Eden Mills Writers' Festival Poetry Contest. Many of the poems in this book exist because of funding from the Ontario Arts Council.

Thank you to the places I've lived: the Anishinaabeg, Cree, Dakota, Dene, Métis, and Oji-Cree lands of the Winnipeg area, Treaty 1 territory, where I was born and raised; the unceded Algonquin lands of Ottawa where I grew into a writer; the Anishinaabeg, Haudenosaunee, Wendat, and Mississauga lands of Toronto, Treaty 13 territory, where I became a poet; and the Anihshininiwag and Anishinaabeg lands of the Sioux Lookout area, Treaty 3 and 9 territories, where I currently live.

Being that this is my first book, I feel that I must thank those who supported me while I was writing these poems, and those who supported my early growth as a writer. Thank you to Dionne Brand and every writer who uses words to defend the dispossessed. Thank you to the In/Words group in Ottawa for making novice writers feel confident and relevant. Thank you to my friends from "the Ron" for supporting Slackline when it happened. Thank you to the *Brick, A Literary Journal* family for valuing me and other young writers. Thank you to the Sioux-Hudson Literacy Council for welcoming me into the clan, for allowing me the flexibility to write, and for the experiences and friendships that now enrich my life. Thank you Raf Finn, Jackson Donnelly, Liz Johnston, Alvin Wong, H. Masud Taj, and Jordan Prato for reading early versions of these poems and offering positive feedback that fired my writing engine. Thank you Allan Hepburn for keeping me in mind. Thank you Laurie D. Graham for your editing eyes, your moral integrity, and your guidance. Thank you to my friends and family, all sides of you, for attempting to understand poetry. Thank you to Sioux Lookout for your people and your beauty. Thank you to all my friends who have passed. And the biggest thanks to Jess, the J in my name.